About Tintagel

Paul White

Bossiney Books · Launceston

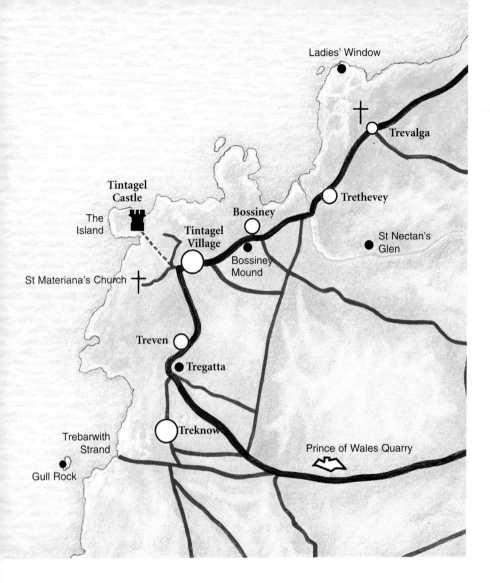

Ladies' Window

Trevalga

Tintagel
Castle

Trethevey

Bossiney

The
Island

Tintagel
Village

St Nectan's
Glen

Bossiney
Mound

St Materiana's Church

Treven

Tregatta

Trebarwith
Strand

Treknow

Prince of Wales Quarry

Gull Rock

First published 2000 by Bossiney Books, Langore, Launceston, Cornwall PL15 8LD
© 2000 Paul White   All rights reserved
ISBN 1-899383-28-X

Acknowledgements
The illustrations are reproduced by kind permission as follows: English Heritage
Photographic Library/Jonathan Bailey page 12; Paul Watts Cornish Picture Library
pages 24, 25 and 31; Royal Institution of Cornwall pages 16 and 23.
Other illustrations from the publishers' own collection.
Photographs taken within Tintagel Castle by kind permission of English Heritage.

Printed in Great Britain by R Booth (Troutbeck Press), Mabe, Cornwall

Introduction

The village of Tintagel and its famous castle attract about half a million visitors every year, but neither village nor castle are quite what they seem.

For a start, Tintagel village was only named Tintagel from around 1890. Before that it was known as Trevena. As hardly anyone had heard of Trevena, and half of Europe had heard of Tintagel because of its famous Arthurian connection, the village's change of name might have been the coup of a marketing genius – except that it had probably occurred slowly and naturally over the previous fifty years.

Historically Tintagel was the name not of the village but of the parish, which is a large one extending from Trethevey (on the far side of Rocky Valley) to Treligga (2 km south of Trebarwith). It was also the name of the castle and the headland on which it stands, which is known as 'The Island' – although the sea has not yet quite detached it from the mainland.

The castle is, in a sense, 'King Arthur's Castle' but in much the same way as the parish church is 'St Materiana's Church'. Both buildings were named in honour of legendary patrons. Neither Saint Materiana nor King Arthur lived in Tintagel; indeed both are shadowy figures who may, or may not, have had a historical existence.

From the middle ages there was a township within the parish of Tintagel which was given the legal status of a borough, and in due course this acquired the right to elect two members of Parliament. By the time of the Great Reform Bill in 1832, Tintagel was a household word as a corrupt 'rotten borough', where a handful of electors – or in 1784 the sole eligible elector! – could be won by bribes or threats.

This book aims to tell you something of the realities of Tintagel rather than its myths, though when I walk on the cliffs here in a winter gale, or on a summer evening, it sometimes seems that the only reality is sea, sky, wind and rock.

Trebarwith Strand in a January gale, with the waves breaking on Penhallic Point. North Cornwall in winter can be very dramatic as well as very beautiful. In these conditions, it is strange to remember that small ships beached here to collect slate from the local quarries

Even if you arrive in Tintagel on a busy day in summer and are surrounded by bemused and noisy crowds milling round the shops and eating places, ten minutes walk will take you to near isolation, the sanity of stunning views of Cornwall's Atlantic coast and scenes of romantic association and genuine historical interest.

Tintagel Castle and the Arthur connection

Until the 1980s, most historians believed that the castle was built around AD 1140, but recent archaeological and historical research has demonstrated that it was in fact not built until 1230-1236. The dates 1140 and 1236 may seem equally remote, but it may have a very important bearing on whether a historical Arthur ever lived at Tintagel.

Looking down from near the summit of the Island onto the Inner Ward (courtyard), where the Great Hall once stood. The building you can see was a late medieval replacement, possibly around 1350. A cliff fall to the right of this building destroyed the medieval defences, and the present outer wall of the ward dates from the Victorian period

The man who paid for the construction of Tintagel Castle was Earl Richard of Cornwall, a younger son of King John. He was in his early twenties at the time, very rich and ambitious, and he knew that Tintagel was the seat of the ancient Dukes of Cornwall, and associated with King Arthur. He 'knew' it because the standard British history book at that time said so. This history was written about 1135 by Geoffrey of Monmouth, who is nowadays usually considered a romancer rather than a historian. We don't believe Geoffrey without firm supporting evidence, but in his time he was regarded as an authority.

About 1230 Richard, Earl of Cornwall, persuaded the owner of the Manor of Bossiney (see page 21), Gervase de Tintajoel, to exchange Bossiney, including Tintagel Island, for two much richer manors elsewhere. This exchange was completed by 1233 – but building work on the castle seems to have started before the lawyers had sorted out the contracts. Nearly eight centuries later, the island and castle remain the property of Earl Richard's successor, the Duchy of Cornwall, but are looked after by English Heritage. There is much to see, and many steps to climb!

In the thirteenth century, there was no conceivable military purpose served by building a castle at Tintagel. There was no road or river crossing to control and enemies arriving by sea would find better landing places elsewhere. It could have served as a defensive refuge, but Richard had no need for that.

The real function of Earl Richard's castle was symbolic. He and his family were to be seen as the true heirs of the great King Arthur, and his castle was proudly sited at what Geoffrey of Monmouth had told the world was the stronghold of the ancient dukes of Cornwall.

Situated half on the mainland and half on the island, with a narrow neck of land between, it was still recognised as virtually impregnable even 200 years after its building when it was already in ruins – for it was soon seen as an expensive 'folly'. Earl Richard himself found a new fantasy game to play, using his wealth to get himself declared 'King of the Romans'.

The great strength of Tintagel Castle as a defensive position was the chasm between the outer defences on the mainland and the inner defences on the Island. This photograph was taken on the island looking back to the outer defences, which are themselves divided into a lower and an upper ward. Both these wards were once bigger, but cliff falls have diminished them in area

The part of the castle on the mainland consists of two 'wards' or courtyards, the higher one being on a natural crag. The lower ward, with the gatehouse, is approached by a narrow path along the side of the hill. This path has been much widened, for ease of tourist access.

*Crenellations in
the Inner Ward*

In Earl Richard's time the 'neck' joining the Island to the mainland was much higher than it is today, but still very narrow. The climb down and up again was perhaps easier, but it was a path very easily defended. By Tudor times the crossing was by means of elm trees, laid as a bridge. The Inner Ward, on the Island, contained a great hall, and was defended by a crenellated curtain wall on the far side against any seaborne landing. These crenellations are so very romantic that it was long believed they were Victorian additions (as are the gate and wall at the top of the steps to the Inner Ward) but it now appears that they are original.

On a lower slope, a further stretch of wall, with a gate in it, defends a deep-water landing place known as the Iron Gate, in Cornish *Porth Hern* – a name which has given rise to much speculation over its origin. The Latin words *portus*, a haven, and *porta*, a gate, both found their way into the ancient British language (which later developed into Cornish/Breton/Welsh) as *porth*. Although *hern* can mean iron in Cornish, it may be a corruption of the local dialect pronunciation of English 'haven', as 'haw'un'.

The castle soon proved too expensive to keep in good repair. The great hall was deliberately unroofed and a smaller building put in its place as a home for a 'constable' – a kind of white-collar caretaker. Most of the castle started to fall into ruins, and before long cliff falls had taken large parts of it into the sea.

Porth Hern, the 'Iron Gate'

The Island before the Castle

It has always been clear that there was a settlement on the Island long before the castle was built. The whole land surface is covered with mounds which are the remains of ancient walls, some of slate, some of turf. But what exactly were they and when were they built?

Excavations in the 1930s under Dr Ralegh Radford, a young man who was later to become an eminent archaeologist, were undertaken to uncover what was believed to be a 'Celtic monastery', and a number of walls were reconstructed to show them more clearly. Archaeology has made huge strides since the 1930s and by modern standards there was a great deal wrong with this under-funded excavation – and even more wrong with the Ministry of Works' subsequent reconstructions.

A series of excavations in the 1990s overturned the 1930s interpretation, although they tackled only a tiny percentage of the Island's land surface and much remains to be done. Professor Charles Thomas in his splendid book *Tintagel: Arthur and Archaeology* (Batsford/English Heritage, 1993) explains the sequence of excavations and discoveries in some detail. The archaeologists have now demonstrated that there never was a monastery here.

In many cases the footings of buildings were probably temporary huts for the castle builders in the 1230s, but some have been shown to be from the fifth and sixth centuries. Associated with these there have been astonishing 'finds'. Vast quantities of fragments of imported pottery have been found, of types which are known to have been made in the eastern Mediterranean and North Africa at that time. These include large numbers of *amphorae* (storage jars used for wine, oil and dry goods) and plates and bowls of high quality.

The amount of such pottery found at Tintagel is actually greater than the total from all other sites in Britain and Ireland put together. In addition a glass vessel from the Cadiz area of Spain has been discovered, and this is unique for the period.

Part of the post-Roman settlement once believed to be a monastery

A carved slate was found in 1998 including the name ARTOGNOV, a British name probably pronounced 'Arthnou'. This caused much delight among local people and is optimistically referred to as 'the Arthur stone', but the scholars are not convinced it has any such significance. It does, however, seem to confirm that a Romanised way of life existed at Tintagel in the sixth century AD, and that the inhabitants used written Latin. (The ancient British tongue, alas, was never written down.)

The excavators ruled out the possibility that Tintagel was a port for wine and pottery importation with a very careless work force, and came to the conclusion that the Island could well have been what the much maligned Geoffrey of Monmouth, and many other Celtic story-tellers, said it was, a seat of the 'Dukes' of Cornwall.

Quite possibly Tintagel is the *Durocornovium* ('the fortress of the Cornovii') enigmatically mentioned by a late Roman writer.

Cornwall in the post-Roman period

Centralised Roman rule in Britain ceased about AD 400 (the date of 410 is often given but is over-precise) and the country broke up into about 25-30 miniature states, each centred on a Roman city and mostly representing tribal units. Modern Cornwall, Devon and parts of Somerset were all part of the state (*civitas*) of Dumnonia, centred on Isca (Exeter) and some 320 km (200 miles) in total length from Scilly to Sedgemoor.

Like many of the other states, Dumnonia became an independent kingdom. Although Devon and Somerset were lost to the Saxons, the Cornish part survived until the ninth century. The names of some of Dumnonia's early kings are known, but in a confused way. The period 400-600 can be described as 'post-Roman'.

Most scholars at present agree that Tintagel was a royal stronghold of the Dumnonians. Probably it was only used in summer: no one in their right mind would choose to live on the Island in a winter gale! They traded something – almost certainly tin – for supplies of Mediterranean wine, oil and luxury goods such as dinner services and glass.

Most kings and powerful aristocrats with widespread estates used to travel about their lands with their retainers, eating the produce of each estate in turn: it was easier for the Court to go to the food than for the food to be brought to the Court. (English monarchs continued to do this at least until 1600.) Perhaps Tintagel was a regular stop on the annual Dumnonian royal itinerary.

Professor Thomas has suggested that a curious footprint-shaped hollow in the rock, known in the nineteenth century as 'King Arthur's footprint', may actually have formed part of a Dumnonian king-making ceremony, for which there are parallels elsewhere in the Celtic world. Perhaps Tintagel was the scene of coronations and ceremonial feasts.

One intriguing possibility is that when Earl Richard built his

'A rocky path which could be defended by three men against an army' – so said Geoffrey of Monmouth, and the path remains to this day, now defended in summer by a lone English Heritage gate-keeper and the occasional maintenance crew

castle, he deliberately planned it to be physically as well as symbolically on the site of the earlier stronghold. Some of the lower courses of the curtain walls appear to be of a different construction, possibly post-Roman. There are indications that the Great Hall was built over the original 'palace' quarters.

One feature, the great ditch near the landward gateway, is certainly ancient. Geoffrey of Monmouth, describing Tintagel, wrote of a narrow rocky path which could be defended by three men against an army. As we now know he was writing 90 years before Earl Richard's castle was built, he was probably describing the remains of the post-Roman stronghold, which were still visible in 1130, and on which Earl Richard chose to build.

King Arthur

Did 'King Arthur' really exist? He was certainly not a figment of Geoffrey's imagination, because there are many references in early Celtic literature to someone called Arthur – though he is not always a king. Sometimes he is a minor chief, sometimes he is a warrior who leads the kings of Britain. He is not always favourably portrayed in these sources and he apparently had little respect for the local saints: the writers were often monks so they may have been biased against him. It is far from clear where he was based: Cornwall is often mentioned, but some suggest he operated in northern Britain.

Readers who are interested in the search for a historical Arthur may care to read my book *King Arthur – man or myth?* which attempts to summarise the evidence.

My own best guess after extensive research – and no one can do more than guess – is that Arthur did exist: that he was not a king but a successful warrior of Dumnonia, perhaps a junior member of the royal family. In his early days he may have been a local chieftain or sub-king at Dunster in North Somerset. Because of his fighting skills he was chosen to lead an army of temporarily united Britons against their enemies, who at that time were likely to have included invaders from Ireland and from south Wales (where modern Dyfed was an Irish colony) as well as Saxons.

As a successful warrior, Arthur became nationally famous – more so than the kings of the time, some of whom were no doubt envious of him as an upstart. But the unity of the Britons was very fragile, and probably ended in warfare between the British kingdoms, in which he died. He was historically far less important than his legend suggests.

Whether this is a true summary of the historical Arthur is not particularly important. What really matters is his status in legend and as a political symbol. Several medieval kings named their eldest sons Arthur, but they all died before they could

*Much the same view seen by a photographer and (opposite)
by an artist – who has romanticised the scene*

inherit the throne. Anglo-Norman invasions of Scotland and
Wales were justified on the dubious grounds that Arthur had
once ruled there. Later a literary fantasy of the grail and the
Knights of the Round Table sustained both genuine idealism
and Victorian imperialism. Whatever the Arthur of history may
have been, the 'real' King Arthur is the Arthur of legend.

Linking Arthur and Tintagel

No reference before Geoffrey of Monmouth (writing around
1135) connects Arthur with Tintagel. Instead, Tintagel is
described as the stronghold of King Mark, a probably legendary
king of Cornwall. Geoffrey says Arthur was conceived at
Tintagel (the most defensible stronghold of Gorlois, Duke of
Cornwall) but never suggests Arthur was born here, or that he
ever visited it again.

William of Worcester (1478) heard that Arthur was conceived *and* born at Tintagel. A government survey in 1650 refers to 'the manor or mansion house commonly known by the name of King Arthur Castle alias Tintagell Castle', but the first written reference to Arthur *residing* at Tintagel is apparently a travel guide dated 1851.

Alfred Lord Tennyson, who visited Tintagel in 1848 and 1860, recreated the Arthur legend in his *Morte d'Arthur* and *Idylls of the King*. Almost equally important in popularising Tintagel was the minor poet and first-rate eccentric Rev Robert Stephen Hawker, rector of Morwenstow, Cornwall's most northerly parish, who wrote *The Quest of the Sangraal* in 1863. He was at the time mourning the death of his first wife and apparently living exclusively on clotted cream and opium, a diet rather appropriate for Victorian effusions on the Arthur theme. (He shortly ended his depression by marrying a second wife 57 years younger than the first.)

Over a period of years, Tintagel people attempted to please visitors by renaming old features. 'Merlin's Cave' was a name invented by Victorian guides. At that time the haven area was quite industrial and a walkway (visible in the photograph on page 16) led to 'King Arthur's Mine' in one of the caves

Tintagel featured strongly in both Tennyson's and Hawker's poems and was in consequence visited by most of the major Victorian writers, from Dickens and Wilkie Collins to Swinburne, and of course by Thomas Hardy, then a young architect restoring the church of St Juliot near Boscastle. He and his fiancée got locked in the castle after hours, which must have been very romantic, and were rescued only after much waving of pocket hankies.

Arthur's final battle at 'Camlann' has in Cornish folklore been located not far from Tintagel, at Slaughter Bridge. This was the historical site of a much later battle between Cornish and Saxons and the two separate events may have been confused in popular memory.

The holiday destination

The immense popularity of Tennyson's poems in particular put Tintagel firmly on the map. The year the *Idylls* were published, 1859, also saw the opening of the through railway route from London to Penzance. Cornwall began to be talked about as a holiday destination, though the north coast had no railway and remained difficult to reach.

The London & South-Western Railway's line reached Camelford in 1893, and a horse bus service connected it to Tintagel three times a day. King Arthur's Castle Hotel was being built on Fire Beacon Cliff, and alarm bells started to ring for those locals and wealthy visitors alike who loved the old Cornwall – isolated, impoverished but wildly beautiful.

The newly formed National Trust bought Barras Nose and later Glebe Cliffs to prevent any further development of Tintagel's wonderful coastline. If the sleepy and quaint little village of Trevena was to become the modern Tintagel, it would at least be developed inland rather than along the coast.

The strategy worked: even in peak holiday times it is still possible to find relative peace only a few minutes away from the bustle in the centre of the village.

When King Arthur's Castle Hotel was built on the cliffs above the haven it was an unwelcome intrusion to regular visitors. Nowadays some visitors are said to believe it is itself Arthur's castle!

The simple Norman church of St Materiana is one of the delights of Tintagel, well worth the walk from the village or the haven

St Materiana's Church

People often ask, why is the church so far from the village? But the real question should be, why is the village so far from the church? – since the church is a hundred years older than the village, and its site is more ancient still.

The present church was built around 1120-1140, probably the third on the site, the first dating from the tenth century. But before that, there was a *lan* – an egg-shaped walled enclosure typical of early Celtic Christian sites – within which were a stone pillar and a graveyard but no church; and even before that, there was a very early Christian graveyard, dating from the time of the Dumnonian royal stronghold, not long after AD 500. Cornish churches are quite often isolated, built at traditionally sacred places before the development of the parish system. The siting of settlements, on the other hand, depended on such mundane factors as shelter from storms, water supply and communications.

The simplicity of the small Norman church of St Materiana is very appealing. In the south transept is what is generally described as a Roman milestone, dating from around AD 250. There are no recognisable remains of well-constructed Roman roads in Cornwall, so its presence is an unsolved puzzle.

Bossiney

At the time of the Norman conquest, the two major settlements of Tintagel were the manors (landed estates) of Treknow and Bossiney, both of which belonged to the monastery at Bodmin. Bossiney was rented to a Saxon, 'Eluui', possibly Elfwy. The population was Cornish-speaking, but the landowners were increasingly Saxons, soon to be dispossessed by Normans.

The rest of the parish consisted of isolated farms, most of them starting with the Cornish word for a farmstead, *tre* or *tref*. The Manor of Bossiney included the whole area of the modern village of Tintagel, together with the Island on which the castle was later built.

Today you can still see, almost opposite the Bossiney Hotel, a mound which is assumed to be the motte of a small castle, probably Norman, but perhaps late Saxon – or even perhaps an ancient barrow later re-used as a motte. It has never been excavated by archaeologists. The settlement near this castle was there long before Trevena was built up, and the two hamlets were separated by green fields until ribbon development joined them in the twentieth century.

The castle mound at Bossiney – older than Tintagel Castle

The medieval Borough

The building of Tintagel Castle inevitably led to the development of a planned settlement outside its walls, where traders could supply the small garrison and its visitors with everything from food to saddlery, and this in due course became the main street of the modern village. Earl Richard granted a charter to his 'Borough of Tintajoel', probably in 1253. The inhabitants were given the same liberties as Dunheved (now Launceston). Liberties is an odd word, but the inhabitants of medieval 'boroughs' were free at a time when most country people were so closely tied to their birthplace that we would today regard them as slaves, so this was a big step for Tintagel. There was a weekly market, and a three-day annual fair.

Although technically now living in a 'town', most of the inhabitants of the two separate settlements of Bossiney and Trevena farmed their strips in the open fields which lay between the Bossiney-Tintagel road and the sea, and many also fished. In 1338 there may have been as many as 158 households, the high point of population, but economic decline had already set in – indeed it was probably only the generous 'liberties' which prevented the town dying earlier, since the castle was little occupied after 1350. John Leland, in the reign of Henry VIII, wrote 'This Bossinny hath been a bygge thing for a fischar toune... A man may see there the ruines of a great numbre of houses.' By 1550 the population of the whole parish was no more than 400.

Yet at a time when the borough was clearly decaying, the Crown decided to give it a mayor and the right to elect two MPs. This was an attempt at vote-rigging. Small Cornish boroughs could not afford the travelling costs and living expenses of sending two MPs to each parliament, so they were obliged to accept the 'help' of a rich patron. The Crown hoped to control the selection of the MPs to give it a majority in parliament.

Bossiney's MPs included Francis Bacon and in 1584 Francis

The village street of Trevena, a photograph believed to have been taken in 1896. The house on the left is the 'Old Post Office'. Notice the new slate roof on the projecting gable, now replaced by one more in keeping with its character. Its purchase by The National Trust preserved this ancient building from any further unsympathetic modernisation – or even destruction – during Tintagel's development boom in the twentieth century

Drake, elected unanimously by nine voters at the behest of the Earl of Bedford. The mayors and corporation members of Tintagel over the centuries doubtless relished their civic pomp, not to mention the preferment for their relatives in the church or navy, which was the usual price of their votes.

They could also rely on a sequence of good dinners and liquid lunches in election week, and on one occasion a ram fetched the rather surprising price of £400 – fifteen years' wages for a farm labourer. The Great Reform Bill of 1832 removed the abuse, and the burghers promptly voted to dissolve the Borough. It had no purpose other than corruption.

The Old Post Office a hundred years on from the previous photograph

At least one building remains to remind us of the medieval borough – the Old Post Office, restored and maintained by The National Trust. It was a 'Letter Receiving Office' from 1844 to 1892, during which time deliveries were made on foot from Camelford. Trevena was selected as a central point within the parish of Tintagel, and this is probably how the village name began to change. (An 1892 guidebook says 'The name of the village, though often called Tintagel, is actually Trevena, the better known name being that of the parish and castle.')

The building is probably fourteenth century. It may have been occupied by a steward looking after the lord's interests in the growing township. Although small, so needing only a brief visit, it is a unique building and an unforgettable experience.

King Arthur's Halls

When the Borough ceased to exist, the town hall and market hall were knocked down and Trevena House was built on the site in the 1860s. In the rear part of Trevena House and in its former garden is one of the most surprising tourist attractions in Cornwall – King Arthur's Great Halls.

These were the creation of Frederick Glasscock, retired manufacturer from Clerkenwell of custard, jellies and 'hundreds-and-thousands'. He had sold his business Monk & Glass and retired to Tintagel by 1920, where his fortune allowed him to indulge an extraordinary dream, recreating the Fellowship of the Round Table – with himself as its leader. It was an enormous success, recruiting at least 17,000 members. The Halls opened in 1933. It is still possible to become a member of the Fellowship.

All this could seem a bit comic, even bizarre, but Glasscock is remembered in the village as a philanthropist and the Halls themselves are actually rather impressive.

The chivalric ideal continues to inspire many who visit.

The workmanship, by Cornish masons using many different local building stones, most noticeably the light grey Polyphant granite, is quite superb. There are fine examples of stained glass by Veronica Whall (Glasscock proved a tricky customer when it came to settling her bill!) and a series of paintings of Arthurian scenes by the late-Victorian artist William Hatherell, still painting in the 1920s

Remnants of a slate quarry on the beautiful clifftop walk from Tintagel Church to Trebarwith Strand

The slate industry

Slate has been quarried commercially in the Tintagel-Delabole area since the fifteenth century. At Delabole it is possible to visit the massive working quarry, but the quarries in Tintagel parish are now silent. Many were along the cliffs, and the coast path from the Island or the church to Trebarwith Strand is thoroughly recommended both for its natural beauty and for the interesting remains of the industry. Look for the platforms and strongpoints on the cliffs, from which 'poppet-heads' (derricks) lowered slate to vessels precariously moored against the cliffs; and for the giant stacks which were left because the low-grade slate was not worth extracting. On the cliff path there are some beautifully constructed hedges (as stone boundary walls are called hereabouts) with intricate herring-bone patterns, and a variety of ingenious stiles.

The National Trust's excellent Tintagel leaflet gives details of the individual quarries.

Trebarwith Strand is at the foot of a valley full of quarries, and trains of pack horses used to carry the slate down to ships beached on the sands. The heavy transport costs of Cornish roofing slate made it very hard for the quarries to compete with their rivals in Wales for the Midland market and with Belgian slate for the London market.

About 2.5km (1.5 miles) up the valley from Trebarwith Strand lies the Prince of Wales quarry, marked by a prominent engine house (restored) which last worked in the nineteenth century. Now it is an informal nature reserve and a very picturesque place to visit.

The restored engine house at the Prince of Wales Quarry, unusual in that its walls are built of slate and not granite. Most Cornish engine houses were built for the mining industry rather than the quarries. Tin and copper were always found in the granite areas of Cornwall, so granite was always available for building, but here slate had to be used instead

The Tintagel area has recently discovered, or perhaps rediscovered, another resource besides slate – the constant wind which is now harvested by wind farms. That at Delabole is open to the public in summer. There are people who find wind farms ugly, but personally I am untroubled by them visually, have never heard one making an excessive noise, and think them a spendid contribution to green energy.

In the same neighbourhood you will find the particularly interesting British Cycling Museum. A little further inland is the legendary site of Arthur's last battle, at Slaughter Bridge.

Rocky Valley and Trevalga

The walk north-east along the coast from the Island towards Boscastle is one of the finest stretches of cliff scenery anywhere in the world. Depending on how strong you feel, you could walk as far as Bossiney Haven, from which a sunken packhorse track leads back up to Bossiney. (The packhorses carried seaweed and sand which were used to improve the fertility of the fields, and perhaps just the occasional keg of brandy or rum.)

Or you could go on further to Rocky Valley, where a stream cuts spectacularly through the cliff to the sea. Halfway up this valley are the remains of a watermill, and just behind it are some mysterious carvings of a maze pattern of Bronze Age origin – though whether the carvings are as old as that is very doubtful. More probably they were the work of a miller with time on his hands when the stream ran low in a drought!

But what does it matter? The sacred symbols are just as effective whenever they were carved, or so it would seem from the offerings left here at what has become a shrine.

The Rocky Valley carvings under scrutiny

The strange rock formation near Trevalga known as the Ladies' Window

If you want a more strenuous walk, further along the coast you reach a rock formation called the Ladies' Window, and inland the little hamlet and church of Trevalga, and beyond that again the ancient strip fields called the Forrabury Stitches, then Boscastle itself. As you walk, you will see ahead of you a strange white building on the Willapark headland above Boscastle. Although once used as a coastguard station, it was probably originally built as both a summer house and a 'daymark' to help shipping trying to identify the entrance to Boscastle.

The waterfall at St Nectan's Kieve. 'Kieve' is an old dialect word for a basin

St Nectan's Kieve

The stream which runs through Rocky Valley has come down a delightful wooded coombe known as St Nectan's Glen. Footpaths give access from Halgabron on the south side of the valley or from the Rocky Valley Centre at Trethevey on the north side, and lead up towards St Nectan's Kieve and waterfall (fee payable at the tea rooms).

This is a strange and romantically beautiful spot, of unique geological and botanical interest. It has an odd atmosphere too and it does not surprise me that those with the ability to see ghosts apparently see more of them here than anywhere else in Cornwall, nor that it should be viewed as 'a potent symbol of Mother Earth… a place of healing and spiritual regeneration'.

The Rev AC Canner, former vicar of Tintagel and author of a history of the parish, seemed to take delight in demolishing the Kieve's historical credentials – perhaps he recognised a potent spiritual rival! The connection with St Nectan was a fabrication by the famous Parson Hawker, who delighted in private jokes.

Hawker had known it as 'Nathan's Cave' in 1830 but later declared with a twinkle in his eye that it had 'borne for ten centuries the name of St Nectan's Kieve' – although other saints real or imaginary such as St Nathan, St Neot and St Knighton had been tried in the meantime, and Dickens when he visited understood it to be St Wightan's Glen.

For me the unfolding story of 'Nathan's Cave' transforming itself into 'St Nectan's Kieve' is rather like the story of Tintagel itself. In an attempt to please the visitor with romantic stories, whether of King Arthur, St Nectan or the 'two grey ladies', local guides and shopkeepers, abetted by writers, have invented or embellished legends which the next generation of local people have come to believe in and to rely on for their livelihood.

In addition to the old Arthur myths we now have 'ley lines' and a newly discovered spiritual significance.

The irony is that Tintagel is so splendid (and St Nectan's Kieve likewise) that they do not need these props on which to sell them. The reality is so much better than the fictions.